The Prestige Series

Yorkshire Traction 2

John Banks

Includes Photography by

G H F Atkins

ISBN-10 1 905304 11 0
ISBN-13 978 1 905304 11 0

Cover: Passing St George's Minster, *en route* to the new Doncaster Interchange, opened beneath the extended Frenchgate Centre in June 2006, No. **449** (**N109 CET**) also carries a Stagecoach name and fleet No. 32933. This Northern Counties Paladin bodied Dennis Dart was new to Yorkshire Terrier in 1995. Note that the combination of digital camera and electronic display has rendered the destination invisible. *(Don Wilson)*

Rear Cover: This East Lancs-bodied Scania Omnidekka carries the blue and yellow Yorkshire Traction livery introduced for low floor buses in 2004. No. **801** (**YN54 VKA**)**,** waiting to depart for Barnsley, stands outside the modernistic terminal building at Robin Hood Airport, Doncaster, which opened in April 2005. *(Don Wilson)*

Inside front cover: Although by now into the early years of the National Bus Company, it was still possible to find vehicles in Yorkshire Traction's traditional red and cream in 1971. No. **728** (**3281 HE**), originally numbered 1281, was a Leyland PD3A/1 with forward entrance Northern Counties body new in October 1964. No. **222** (**NHE 22F**) on the other hand, a 1967 Alexander Y type-bodied Leyland Leopard PSU3/4R had already succumbed to the NBC's so called 'dual-purpose' white/red colour scheme. *(Both: Geoffrey Weston)*

Inside rear cover: Seen here in the first version of the NBC's poppy red and white is Leyland National No. **403** (**FHE 403L**), which was new in 1973 and was photographed two years later. *(G H F Atkins/© John Banks Collection)* New some 30 years later, No. **221** (**YT03 AYF**), a MAN 14.220 with East Lancs Myllennium body has received corporate Stagecoach livery and new fleet number three years after delivery. In the background steel framing for the new bus station can be seen. *(Don Wilson)*

Title page: Leyland Olympian No. **602** (**NKU 602X**), a 1981 Eastern Coach Works 77-seater, entered service in December that year wearing a livery commemorating the Company's 80 anniversary. *(G H F Atkins/© John Banks Collection)*

Below: A line up of, from right to left, Nos. **402-6** (**J402-6 XHL**), Reeve Burgess-bodied 41-seat Dennis Darts, at Barnsley depot in September 1992. *(Geoff Coxon)*

» *Opposite page:* The move into National Bus Company control inevitably saw the eventual suppression of Yorkshire Traction's traditional red and cream livery, a particularly grievous loss in the case of the express coaches, which emerged in a less than imaginative all-over white. Being given a wash and brush up in this 1978 view was 1972's No. 27 (BHE 27K), a 49-seat Plaxton-bodied Leyland PSU3B/4R Leopard. *(Geoff Coxon)*

THE YORKSHIRE TRACTION
COMPANY LIMITED

YORKSHIRE TRACTION CO.
UPPER SHEFFIELD ROAD
BARNSLEY
S70 4PP

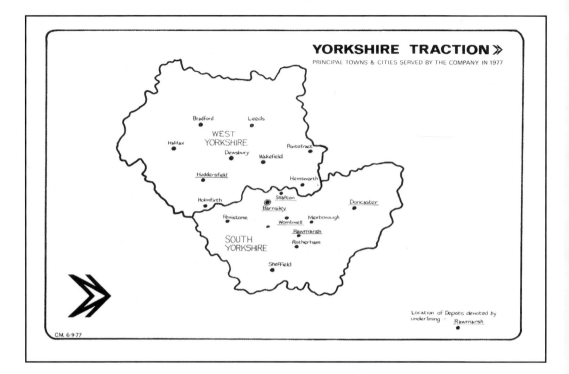

YORKSHIRE TRACTION »
PRINCIPAL TOWNS & CITIES SERVED BY THE COMPANY IN 1977

INTRODUCTION

In 2000 Venture Publications Ltd, as No. 5 in its then relatively new Prestige Series, issued an illustrated survey of the Yorkshire Traction fleet using the photography of the late G H F Atkins, with text and captions by the present writer. That book concentrated on the period approximately 1930 to 1968, that is to say those years during which Yorkshire Traction was a BET constituent in which, nevertheless, the railways - and then the British Transport Commission (BTC) following nationalisation in 1948 and then the Transport Holding Company (THC) from 1963 - had a substantial shareholding. In 2002 Yorkshire Traction celebrated its centenary and then on 15th December 2005, as part of the Traction Group, was purchased by Stagecoach.

The present volume revisits the golden era of the halfcab, advances the story with a look at events in the years since 1969, among them the National Bus Company (NBC), deregulation and privatisation, and concludes with the first outward evidence of Stagecoach in early 2006. It is hoped that a further volume will expand the coverage of those relatively recent parts of the Company's long and honourable history, as well as bringing the new Stagecoach régime into clearer focus: at the time of writing there are already momentous changes afoot concerning the engineering headquarters at Upper Sheffield Road, Barnsley, and once Stagecoach has "settled in" there will doubtless be, after a further year or so, much to report.

The Growth of the Company

Yorkshire Traction had been born as a result of the Barnsley & District Light Railways Order, 1900, as a consequence of which the British Electric Traction Company Ltd (BET), in March 1902, registered a company then known as the Barnsley & District Electric Traction Company Ltd, which ran trams on the Worsbrough and Smithies routes from November 1902 to August 1930. Although many other routes were contemplated, and for which the Company possessed the necessary powers, no others were ever initiated.

The reason was not far to seek; in October 1912 the Company had taken its first steps to becoming a motorbus user, starting modestly in that month with an order for five Brush-bodied Leylands. By 1925 it had a fleet of 118 and the word "Electric" was dropped from its title, which in 1929 was changed to the Yorkshire Traction Company Ltd. The introductory notes to the 2000 volume described how the railways

<< Opposite page: The Yorkshire Traction operating area in 1977 when the National Bus Company had become well established following its formation on 1st January 1969. *(John Banks Collection/Yorkshire Traction)*

Above and below: For the commencement of motorbus services the first vehicles came in 1913 and were all Leyland S models with 27-seat front-entrance bodywork by Brush, of Loughborough. There were two batches, Nos 1-5 delivered in the May and Nos 6-10 in the September. The picture of No. **3** (**HE 10**) of the first batch *(above)* shows, with his foot on the entrance step, Mr P H Marco, the manager of the company, which at that time was proudly signwritten as The Barnsley & District Electric Traction Co. Ltd, reflecting its tramway origins and operations. From the second batch is illustrated No. **7** (**HE 46**). *(Both: John Banks Collection)*

sought powers to operate motorbuses in their own right and how the LMSR and the LNER bought in to Yorkshire Traction becoming equal shareholders with the Tilling & British Automobile Traction Co. Ltd. In 1942, when Tilling and BET operations were divided, Yorkshire Traction became a BET company. The railway-owned shares were nationalised in 1948 and in 1963 passed to the THC, the successor to the Tilling organisation. Thus the THC had shares in the BET-owned Yorkshire Traction.

On 1st January 1969, following the BET's sell-out to the THC in the previous year, the National Bus Company, of mixed recollection, lurched into being and one of its constituent companies was Yorkshire Traction.

Under NBC auspices it at first continued much as before. There was participation in National Express and National Holidays activity and in 1974, following the creation of the Metropolitan Counties of South and West Yorkshire, the Company's stage carriage network, which fell into and across the new boundaries, was coordinated with those of the respective Passenger Transport Executives.

When the NBC was privatised in 1985 a successful buy-out by management, led by Managing Director Frank Carter, brought Yorkshire Traction back into private ownership on 28th January 1987. In 1988 the Lincolnshire Road Car Company was purchased from the remnants of the NBC, and the Newark operator W Gash & Sons was acquired shortly afterwards. The Gash operation was immediately absorbed into the subsidiary Lincolnshire Road Car. Ridings Travel was bought from Caldaire Holdings, also in 1988.

In 1990 the business of Tom Jowitt, of Tankersley, was acquired and in effect converted to a so-called "low-cost" unit under the identity Barnsley & District Traction Co. Ltd. This was ostensibly to compete with other operators.

The Scottish Bus Group was also disbanded as was the NBC, and Yorkshire Traction added Strathtay Scottish (founded in 1985) to its empire in 1990, becoming the only company south of the border to take on a piece of the former Scottish Bus Group. Somewhat ironically, in view of 2005's Stagecoach takeover, the Strathtay move a decade and a half earlier threw Traction into direct competition with Stagecoach in Eastern Scotland and there was some realignment of operations as a

consequence, concentrating activity in and around Dundee. In 1993 Meffan of Northmuir was acquired by the Strathtay subsidiary, but retained its identity.

In 1991 the Barnsley area activities of Shearings were acquired and the following year saw the Kirton Lindsey operator Barnard subsumed into Road Car. The breakthrough into Sheffield came with the purchase of Andrews of Sheffield, which was kept on as a subsidiary and which then absorbed South Riding in 1993 as well as Basichour (Sheffield Omnibus) and Yorkshire Terrier in 1995. The resultant Andrews unit was then renamed Andrews Sheffield Omnibus, which was used for a time as a fleetname and remains the legal identity, though the fleetname is now Yorkshire Terrier.

Lincoln City Transport, privatised in 1991 through a combination of an employee buy-out and a major shareholding by Derby City Transport, was purchased by Traction Group in 1993.

In 1999 a short-lived foothold in the Capital via a stake in London Traveller was acquired; following a reorganisation and renaming to Metropolitan Omnibus (London) it ceased to trade in 2002.

Although Eagre, of Gainsborough, kept its coaching operations, its bus activities passed to the Group in early 2002 and were at once incorporated into the Road Car operation - logically, as Road Car already had a depot in the town.

There could well be some sorting out to do with regard to the monopolies and mergers aspect of the Stagecoach acquisition. Other potential purchasers having withdrawn, it has fallen to Brian Souter's empire to add to its portfolio a thriving and far-flung group with 850 vehicles and an operating area which may conflict with existing Stagecoach activity.

Vehicle Policy

From the start Leyland was the favoured supplier of motorbus chassis. The earliest, delivered in 1913/4, were S types with bodywork by Brush, from whom the Barnsley & District Electric Traction Co. Ltd, as the Company was then titled, had purchased electric tramcars in 1902/3 and 1912. Although some of the 1913 vehicles were withdrawn in 1915, the majority lasted well into the 1920s, the last not

Photographed when new in March 1923, carrying a simplified version of the Barnsley & District fleetname transfer, is No. **75** (**HE 1645**), a Leyland G7 with Brush 28-seat bodywork. Externally there was little apparent difference to show for a decade of development between 1913's solid-tyred Brush-bodied 27-seater seen on page five and the 1923 vehicle shown here. This is especially significant when it is recalled that that decade had unleashed upon the world the 1914-18 war - the "Great War" as it came to be known - a conflict that saw mechanised transport largely supplant the horse as a means of moving troops and hauling guns and other impedimenta for inflicting carnage and destruction. The thrust given to designers and builders by the demands of the military in those circumstances saw improvements and refinements of specification and efficiency that, as is always the way in such things, often did not become available until after the end of hostilities; nevertheless, they perhaps would have taken longer to emerge had the war not taken place and, in fact, the 1923 vehicle was a good deal more sophisticated than its 1913 predecessor and was but a step away from the Leyland Lion with its pneumatic tyres and "modern" halfcab layout: a specification that would remain essentially the standard until the underfloor-engined single-decker appeared as a practical proposition after the Second World War. *(Both: John Banks Collection)*

going until 1927 - a good age for a bus in those rough and ready pioneering days.

Once the First World War was over the fleet was rapidly augmented, initially with Leyland N types in 1919-21, then RAF types in 1922/3, SG7s in 1924 and Z7s in 1925.

The last of the pre-Rackham designs, and perhaps the only pre-Rackham Leyland to achieve "classic" status - was the PLSC1 Lion, soon to be augmented by the longer PLSC3. Yorkshire Traction bought its first Lions in 1926 and many more through the rest of the twenties and into the thirties as the model was developed and improved into the LT range.

In common with many another larger operator in the 1920s, the Company acquired other businesses as the opportunity arose, and by this means added further Leylands as well as a variety of non-standard chassis to its fleet, including AEC, ADC, Berliet, Chevrolet, Dennis, GMC, Gotfredson, Guy, Karrier, Lancia, Reo, Star and Thornycroft. Some of these, especially the Leylands, were used for a year or two but the majority were quickly withdrawn and sold; some, indeed, were not allocated fleet numbers and may not have been used before being sold.

Leyland, Ransomes, Strachan & Brown and Hall, Lewis received orders for coachwork in this period, although Brush was not entirely eclipsed.

As the new decade moved on Leyland strengthened its hold on the fleet with double-deck Titans and single-deckers on the Lion and Tiger chassis. One of the glories of the Yorkshire Traction fleet was its fine series of Leyland Tiger coaches. The list of coachbuilders patronised expanded in the 1930s to include Burlingham, Eastern Coach Works, Metro-Cammell, Roe, Short Brothers and Weymann with Brush again hanging on with a few orders.

Somewhat unexpectedly, new chassis were bought from other than Leyland in the early part of the decade, with Daimler and Dennis both receiving substantial orders, but by 1935 things had settled down and only Leylands were bought new until the enforced ordering of Guy Arabs after the start of the Second World War. That is not to say that there was not a great deal of variety in the immediate prewar fleet, for second-hand purchases brought in further examples from the miscellany quoted above plus AJS, Albion, Gilford, Maudslay, Renault.

The war wreaked havoc with passenger transport operations, as it did in most other aspects of daily life in Britain and overseas. Bus operators were hit from two sides at once, being called upon to run extra services and augment existing ones for munitions workers and other essential requirements, while at the same time being unable to obtain sufficient new vehicles.

All bus production was immediately frozen by government diktat but after not too long it was realised that little was being served by denying operators new vehicles that had been stopped in mid build or which could be constructed from pre-existing stocks of parts. Thus was born that group of buses that ever since have been known as "the unfrozens". These were essentially to peacetime standards, had a variety of bodies and did not necessarily go to the operators that had ordered them and were merely a palliative, which scarcely dented the problem of vehicle shortages.

That problem was tackled by the Ministry of Supply issuing an austere specification for bus chassis and bodies, a specification to which vehicle- and coachbuilders were obliged to adhere: an obligation sometimes evident more in the breach than the observance - it is difficult, for example, to bring to mind an example of a Ministry of Supply specification body built by East Lancashire Coachbuilders.

Guy Motors, and later Bristol and Daimler, were allowed to build chassis for double-deckers, and Bedford with the OWB catered for the small single-decker. Coachbuilders turning out these austere, angular and not very comfortable bodies are too numerous to list and the whole subject of the wartime programme has been more fully dealt with elsewhere. Operators could not simply place an order. They had to request an allocation, seldom receiving what they would ideally have preferred by way of quantity or specification.

As the programme of allocations affected Yorkshire Traction, however, we can note that an "unfrozen" Leyland Titan TD7 was allocated in 1942 and 21 Guy Arabs in 1943-5. No fewer than five different makes of bodywork were found on these 21 chassis - Roe, Weymann, Massey, Park Royal and Northern Counties.

Peacetime conditions were again established in 1945 and Yorkshire Traction once more made a wholehearted commitment to Leyland, buying many batches of Tigers and Titans, Royal Tigers

Upper: The Leyland Z types were acquired to counter competitive operators' use of light, fast vehicles, and also to meet the 5-ton weight restriction on many of the bridges in the operating area. Number **117** (**HE 2328**) was a Z7 with Ransomes 20-seat bodywork, new in 1925.

Centre: **HE 2718** (fleet number **138**) was one of the first PLSC1 Lions built by Leyland. It was new in April 1926 and its Brush body was replaced with a 30-seat unit built by Leyland in 1929. This rebodying caused a fleet number change to 265.

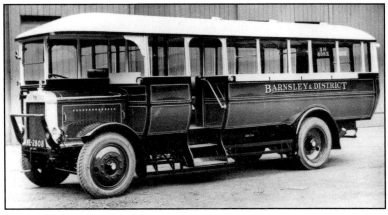

Lower: A slightly later PLSC1 Lion, dating from June 1926, was No. **143** (**HE 2808**), fitted with 30-seat Brush bodywork. Of the 21 PLSC1s bought in 1926, none remained in the fleet after 1936. *(All: John Banks Collection)*

9

and Tiger Cubs. As a consequence of Leyland's bulging order book and its difficulties in meeting it, and in an echo of the early 1930s, during 1949 and 1950 some Dennis Lancets appeared, both as coaches and as service-buses.

Postwar orders for coachwork tended to be less of a monopoly, and vehicles in the fleet could be seen with bodies built by Beadle, Brush, Burlingham, Leyland, Metro-Cammell, NCB, Plaxton, Roe, Saunders, Weymann, Willowbrook and Windover. An interesting feature of Traction's early postwar vehicle policy was the rebuilding of a number of Leyland Tiger single-deckers with new double-deck bodies.

The underfloor- and rear-engined revolutions found an enthusiastic supporter in Traction, with many Leyland Leopards, Leyland Atlanteans and Daimler Fleetlines entering service in the 1960s and in the following decade it was the turn of the Leyland National and the Bristol VR respectively as standard single- and double-deckers. The Leyland Tiger took over from the Leopard for coaches and the Leyland Olympian from the Bristol VR.

The modern Traction Group, from its formation right up to the Stagecoach takeover, has not been a "standardised" fleet. Many of its vehicles have been second-hand, and not only those coming with acquired operators. The Barnsley & District, Road Car and Strathtay fleets have regularly had vehicles transferred to them from the main fleet. More than 50% of the Group total in December 2005 had come second-hand and only the main Yorkshire Traction fleet could boast a majority of vehicles bought new.

Acknowledgements and Author's Afterword

As so often with these *Prestige Series* books, the writer has, through the selfless assistance of a number of friends and enthusiasts, been guided towards making this volume a lot better than it might otherwise have been. On this occasion, again as so often before, Ron Maybray has been ever-patient at the end of the telephone fielding a variety of queries of which even the most abstruse has not baffled him for long; Ken Braithwaite has spent hours looking into details of locations and livery variations and other matters for the captions to such effect that he really ought to be on the cover as joint author; Mary and Dave Shaw have again read the proofs: grateful thanks to all. The illustrations are all from the writer's collection. It has been a joy to make available further examples of Geoffrey Atkins's peerless photography, as well as some of Geoff Coxon's.

Again as so often before, acknowledgement is due to The PSV Circle, whose two-volume fleet history of Yorkshire Traction has proved invaluable; also of help have been "Yorkshire Traction 1902-1977 - 75 Years of Public Service", compiled by C and J R Moyes, and "Yorkshire Traction Early Development" by J A Sykes, published by the Company respectively in 1977 and 1982.

After some seven years or so, this is the last Venture book under the writer's auspices as Series Editor: the end of an era, towards the success of which much blood, sweat and tears have been spilled, but there has also been satisfaction and pleasure in fair proportion. To all those who have stuck with me along the often tricky - sometimes all but impassable - way, profound gratitude: you didn't get a lot out of it but I hope that you have shared my happiness with the results. A few who were involved in the Prestige saga are sadly no longer with us: one thinks of Mike Lockyer, Keith Healey and Geoff Coxon - and Geoffrey Atkins himself, who died on 1st April 2006 at the age of 94 not long after the writer's last visit to him, during which I was moved to see the old chuckle and apposite comment emerge as some photograph or anecdote brought back a transport-related memory. Geoffrey had a little while before that been recognised by Guinness World Records for his achievement in having taken published transport photographs in nine consecutive decades, from 1927 to 2004. For Geoffrey and the others mentioned, *The Prestige Series Nos 1 to 36* among other books stand as our offering to the enthusiast reader.

John Banks
Romiley, Cheshire
June 2006

An enduring feature of the coverage available to us of Yorkshire Traction's prewar operations is the unique series of 1930s Geoffrey Atkins portraits of its Leyland Tiger coaches on Yorkshire Services express workings to and from London as they passed through Nottingham. Traction had a succession of TS2, TS4, TS6, TS7 and TS8 Tiger models, the majority bought new, through the decade. On this page are two Weymann-bodied TS4s, quoted as 28- or 32-seaters in different sources, of June 1932, whose interiors were finished by Burlingham. The photographs of Nos **360/4** (**HE 5637/41**) date from August 1933 and were taken to emphasise a livery variation, in which No. 360 has a single coach line compared with No. 364's double, as well as lacking the cream stripe on the bonnet side. *(Both: G H F Atkins/© John Banks Collection)*

Above: Already by the turn of the decade from the 1920s to the 1930s well established as a regular purchaser of Leyland chassis, Yorkshire Traction was not slow to order the latest versions of the various models as they came on to the market. The PLSC models of the Leyland Lion gave way to the LT1 in 1930 in the Traction fleet and the LT2 came the following year as a batch of 18 Leyland-bodied 30-seaters (338-55), of which No. 348 (**HE 5232**) is seen in Sheffield on the jointly operated (with Sheffield Corporation) service to Huddersfield.

Below: Although Yorkshire Traction is perhaps automatically thought of as "a Leyland fleet", it was not entirely stocked with the Lancashire vehicle builder's products. In 1932, for example, there was a Daimler double-decker and in 1933 Daimler and Dennis single-deckers, in each case bodied by Brush, appeared, of which we are fortunate to have fine portraits in as-built condition. The Daimlers were six magnificent 28-seat coaches on the CP6 chassis. Representing Nos 367-72 is No. 369 (**HE 5992**), which was delivered to Traction in May 1933. *(Both: John Banks Collection)*

Above: The Dennises, also in May 1933, were three Lancet I 32-seat service buses, Nos 373-5, of which the second, No. **374** (**HE 5997**), is shown. *(John Banks Collection)*

Below: A further 20 Dennis Lancet I service buses appeared in 1934, although the bodywork orders went to Roe (19) or Metro-Cammell (1), rather than Brush. A Roe example, No. **407** (**HE 6320**), features in a September 1935 scene at Doncaster railway station. It was about to leave for Huddersfield on what was at that time a through service via Barnsley. *(G H F Atkins/© John Banks Collection)*

Above: Two aspects of the Yorkshire Services Bradford to London express operation are contrasted on this page. In August 1935 at Huntingdon Street bus station, Nottingham, one of Geoffrey Atkins's incomparable portraits gives us No. **429** (**HE 6342**) as it waited to resume the journey northwards after a refreshment stop. The chassis was a Leyland Tiger TS6 and the 28-seat coachwork by Eastern Coach Works. The vehicle had been new in May 1934.

Below: The dappled, tranquil, traffic-free surroundings near Bunny on the approaches to Loughborough frame a Bradford to London coach on a journey in July 1936. Number **549** (**HE 7147**) was a Leyland Tiger TS7c, new the previous May, fitted with a Burlingham 31-seat coach body. *(Both: G H F Atkins/© John Banks Collection)*

Above: Each reader will have his own idea of what constituted Yorkshire Traction's "golden age". For some it will be the mid 1930s, that pathetically short period when the difficulties of the depression were gradually being overcome but which was overshadowed by the threat of another war. Vehicles of the era certainly had "something", as shown by this immaculately prepared Brush-bodied Leyland TD3c highbridge 53-seater, No. **438** (**HE 6654**), seen when brand new in March 1935. The "c" in the model designation indicated "torque converter", an early form of automatic transmission that - on this vehicle - was removed in 1940 and replaced by a manual gearbox. The bus was rebodied by Strachans in 1946.

Below: Standards were as high in May 1939 when Roe-bodied 32-seat Leyland Tiger TS8 No. **640** (**HE 8930**) was photographed before delivery. *(Both: John Banks Collection)*

The phenomenon of the wartime "austerity", or "utility" bus, built to a specification laid down by the Ministry of Supply to a spartan standard that attempted to eschew all curves, frills and comfort, is well known, as is the procedure under which operators had to apply to the Ministry of War Transport for an allocation of new vehicles. These necessarily unattractive but characterful vehicles are represented in our survey of the Yorkshire Traction fleet by *(above)* a lowbridge example, No. **764L (HE 9889)**, bodied as a 55-seater by Roe; and *(below)* by highbridge No. **724H (HE 9978)**, which was a 56-seater bodied by Northern Counties. Both were Guy Arab IIs, delivered into the fleet respectively in August 1944 and April 1945 and both were photographed at Barnsley in the mid 1950s. *(Both: G H F Atkins/© John Banks Collection)*

Above: Many operators rebodied wartime austerity buses after the bodywork had been found less durable than the chassis, and Yorkshire Traction was no exception. Originally bodied by Massey, this 1943 Guy Arab II was rebodied as a lowbridge 55-seater by Roe in November 1950. Number **709** (**HE 9806**) was photographed in June 1951 on a Grimethorpe Red City service. The letters "LB" alongside the destination screen denoted the vehicle's lowbridge specification.

Below: Prewar chassis were also frequently rebodied. Among those done by Traction was No. **577** (**HE 7773**), a 1937 Leyland Tiger TS7, whose original Burlingham coachwork was replaced by this Roberts 34-seat service-bus body in February 1948. It is seen at Wath upon Dearne on service 23 from Barnsley to Thurnscoe, which followed the route of the former Dearne District Light Railway. *(Both: G H F Atkins/© John Banks Collection)*

Above: Another wartime delivery had been No. **664** (**HE 9518**). New in January 1940, this Leyland Titan TD5 had an Eastern Coach Works 54-seat highbridge body. It was photographed on a Barnsley local service in August 1953.

Below: The early postwar standard double-decker in all-Leyland form is represented by highbridge 56-seater No. **834** (**BHE 764**), an April 1950 Titan PD2/1. This picture was taken in April 1962 and shows the vehicle leaving Barnsley bus station for Kexborough, a location somewhat abbreviated on the destination blind. *(Both: G H F Atkins/© John Banks Collection)*

Above: Dennis chassis appeared in the fleet in the early postwar period to augment the Leylands at a time when Leyland was having difficulty fulfilling its order book. Yorkshire Traction had Lancets as coaches and as service buses, of which No. **863** (**CHE 355**), a May 1950 delivery, is seen in Barnsley bus station in June 1951. The 32-seat bodywork was by Brush.

Below: CHE 379 was fleet number **876**, a coach version of the Dennis Lancet with 33-seat Windover coachwork. It was new in September 1949 and is seen at Derby in July 1952. *(Both: G H F Atkins/© John Banks Collection)*

Above: Although Geoffrey Atkins had plenty of opportunity to see and photograph Yorkshire Traction vehicles on express services in Nottingham, the sight of one on delivery from the coachbuilder added a little variety. Number **822** (**BHE 752**) was a Leyland Tiger PS1 with Brush 32-seat bodywork. It was new, and photographed, in June 1949.

Below: A similar vehicle on more usual duties, seen passing through Sherwood in April 1950 on its way to Doncaster, was No. **895** (**CHE 729**). *(Both: G H F Atkins/© John Banks Collection)*

Above: Leyland Tiger PS2/3 with Windover 32-seat coachwork No. **897** (**CHE 852**) was new in May 1950. In this picture it had paused at Derby bus station in May 1955 on a Yorkshire Services express timing to Birmingham. In August 1960 the chassis was rebodied as a 63-seat double-decker by Northern Counties, becoming No. 1187 (THE 187) *(later renumbered 783 - see inside front cover)*. The Windover body was acquired by Dan Smith of Darfield and placed on a Foden PVSC6 chassis and passed to Yorkshire Traction again, but was not used, when the Smith business was taken over in March 1962.

Below: Also at Derby on a Birmingham express is somewhat more lowly No. **921** (**DHE 352**), a Brush-bodied 43-seat Leyland Royal Tiger. This is a June 1954 photograph. *(Both: G H F Atkins/© John Banks Collection)*

Above: Windover coachwork was pleasantly exotic in what were, in June 1951, still rather austere times following the end of the Second World War. This centre-entrance 37-seat example was mounted on a Leyland Royal Tiger chassis and the resultant vehicle became Yorkshire Traction No. **925** (**DHE 563**). The April 1953 picture was taken in Nottingham's Huntingdon Street bus station and shows the vehicle on a Yorkshire Services express journey.

Below: Leyland Tiger TS8 No. 629 of May 1939 was rebuilt as a Leyland-Beadle coach, taking the new fleet number **972** and being reregistered **EHE 382**. It was at Grantham in July 1952 a few days after delivery into the fleet. (*Both: G H F Atkins/© John Banks Collection*)

Above: Leyland Tiger Cub No. **1023** (**GHE 23**) was new in June 1954 fitted with Saunders-Roe of Beaumaris, Anglesey, 44-seat bodywork. Although a stage-carriage specification vehicle, in this July 1954 view at Nottingham it had been pressed into service on Yorkshire Services express work.

Below: Number **981L** (**EHE 928**), seen in September 1953 at Doncaster's Waterdale bus station, was a Northern Counties-bodied 55-seat lowbridge Leyland Titan PD2/12 that had been new only the previous March. *(Both: G H F Atkins/© John Banks Collection)*

Above: On this page is presented a remarkable contrast in high-capacity double-decker design in vehicles photographed in Yorkshire Traction service a mere eight years apart. Leyland Atlantean PDR1/1 No. **1161** (**RHE 811**), which had a Weymann lowbridge 73-seat body, was new in December 1959 and photographed in Barnsley bus station in April 1960. It was one of the first of Yorkshire Traction's modern high-capacity buses.

Below: In sharp contrast is 60-seater No. **127H** (**DT 9642**), a Roe-bodied Leyland TT5c Titanic that had been new to Doncaster Corporation in February 1938. It passed to W A Cawthorne of Barugh in August 1949, and to YTC in March 1952 on the acquisition of Cawthorne's stage-carriage licence. The photograph, taken in Barnsley bus station in August 1952, shows the vehicle working on the former Cawthorne service to Woolley Colliery. (*Both: G H F Atkins/© John Banks Collection*)

Above: The two vehicles on this page were acquired with the business of Camplejohn Bros of Darfield in January 1961. **TTC 882** was an Atkinson CPL745H and was originally a demonstrator when built in July 1954. It passed to Camplejohn in December 1955 and would become Yorkshire Traction **131c**. The 44-seat service-bus bodywork was by Burlingham.

Below: Ex-Camplejohn No. **130c** (**LWT 880**) was an all-Sentinel STC6 44-seater that had been new to Camplejohn in June 1952. It was photographed in the yard at Yorkshire Traction's Upper Sheffield Road, Barnsley, depot. *(Both: John Banks Collection)*

Above: The business of Dan Smith of Darfield was acquired in March 1962. The only ex-Smith vehicle to be used by Traction was No. **136** (**NDA 14**), a Burlingham-bodied 41-seat Guy Arab UF. The vehicle had been new in June 1954 to Don Everall of Wolverhampton. It was photographed in August 1962 in Nottingham on a Yorkshire Services working.

Below: The fleet was renumbered in 1967, blocks of numbers being allocated to vehicle types. Number **744** (**CHE 315C**) had previously been 1315. It was a Leyland PD3A/1 Titan with Roe 73-seat body new in May 1965. It features in a busy Barnsley scene in June 1968. The Town Hall dominates the background and the bus is about to enter the bus station from Regent Street. *(Both: G H F Atkins/© John Banks Collection)*

Above: The former No. 1243 (**YHE 243**), as renumbered **794**, was a Leyland Tiger rebodied in April 1963 as a 63-seat double-decker by Northern Counties. The chassis was originally Yorkshire Woollen District 707. A new style of block-capital fleetname accompanied the renumbering.

Below: Leyland Titan **744** (**CHE 315C**), which we saw on the previous page in traditional livery, had by May 1974 been repainted in the early NBC scheme. It was in Barnsley bus station about to leave for Doncaster. *(Both: G H F Atkins/© John Banks Collection)*

Above: Management of County Motors (Lepton) Ltd passed to Yorkshire Traction on 1st October 1968 and the vehicles owned at that time were renumbered into the Yorkshire Traction fleet. County No. **95** (**OVH 606**), a Leyland Tiger Cub with Willowbrook 43-seat bodywork, was new in March 1959. It is seen here on private hire work. It became Yorkshire Traction No. 594.

Below: County No. **103** (**YCX 538**) was a Willowbrook-bodied 53-seat Leyland Leopard new in August 1963 that became Yorkshire Traction No. 391. It was waiting in Wakefield bus station to return to Huddersfield. *(Both: Geoff Coxon)*

Above: The Mexborough & Swinton Traction Company was absorbed by Yorkshire Traction on 1st October 1969 and, as with the County vehicles, buses were renumbered into the YTC fleet. Leyland Tiger Cub No. **592** (**YWT 57**) was a Weymann-bodied 42-seater that had been new in 1960 as M & S No. 57. It was photographed in Sheffield in March 1970.

Below: A line of four of the Leyland Atlanteans that replaced the Mexborough system's trolleybuses, photographed at the former M & S Rawmarsh depot, illustrates from left to right Yorkshire Traction Nos **693/2** (**8414/3 YG**) and **682/0** (**7006/4 WU**). The pairs of buses had been new in November 1962 (693/2 as M & S 14/3) and February 1961 (682/0 as M & S 6/4). *(Both: G H F Atkins/© John Banks Collection)*

Above: Another ex-Mexborough & Swinton vehicle was No. **19** (**EWW 108C**) seen here at Blackpool in 1975. The Leyland Leopard chassis was fitted with Duple 49-seat coachwork and the vehicle had been new as M & S No. 108 in April 1965. *(Geoff Coxon)*

Below: A batch of five Park Royal-bodied 76-seat Daimler Fleetlines was ordered by British Rail for 1971 delivery but was diverted to Yorkshire Traction as fleet numbers 752-6 after the NBC took over the bus operating interests of British Rail. The penultimate member of the batch, No. **755** (**XHE 755J**) was photographed when about three months old in June 1971 in Barnsley. *(G H F Atkins/© John Banks Collection)*

Above: The next vehicle numerically in this batch of Daimler Fleetlines is seen after repaint into National Bus Company poppy red and white. Number **756** (**XHE 756J**) was in Barnsley bus station in May 1974 between service runs.

Below: In a June 1971 picture of the railway station parking ground in Barnsley the vehicles include No. **235** (**YHE 235J**), a Leyland Leopard 49-seater with handsome Alexander coachwork. *(Both: G H F Atkins/© John Banks Collection)*

Above: Number **237** (**YHE 237J**) of the same batch but now carrying NBC "local coach" livery was photographed in July 1978 waiting in Midland Street, Barnsley, for its departure time for Ryhill.

Below: Among the last vehicles to be delivered new in the traditional Yorkshire Traction livery of red and cream were Nos **26/8** (**BHE 26/8K**), Leyland Leopard coaches with 49-seat Plaxton bodies. New in March 1972, they are seen inside Victoria Coach Station in the following September. *(Both: G H F Atkins/© John Banks Collection)*

Above: The railway station parking ground was the location for this picture of Leyland Leopard No. **522** (**WHE 522J**). New in January 1971, the vehicle was bodied as a 45-seater by Willowbrook.

Below: A busy scene of buses unloading in Midland Street, Barnsley, in August 1984. Nearest the camera is No. **807** (**FHE 807L**), a Bristol VRTSL6G with Eastern Coach Works 77-seat bodywork new in February 1973 and now sporting the later NBC logo. The other bus is No. **821** (**GAK 481N**), a similar combination dating from November 1974. (*Both: G H F Atkins/© John Banks Collection*)

The Leyland National was a phenomenon that has not quite come to be regarded as "phenomenal". Intended as the standard vehicle that the major operators would more or less be obliged to buy, it was expected to change the British bus landscape by doing away with the double-decker. Revolutionary though it was in many aspects of its design and body construction and generally in the long run proving a sound investment, especially after mechanical problems had been sorted and such things as Gardner engines made available, it never proved to be quite the giant-killer that had been anticipated. Two decades out of production and now itself a part of the past, some are still running at the time of writing and others are preserved. Back in the days when it was making its mark, we see early Yorkshire Traction examples Nos **403/5** (**FHE 403L** and **NHE 405M**) at Barnsley respectively in June 1975 and July 1978. *(Both: G H F Atkins/© John Banks Collection)*

Above: Clean and smart, but not very flatteringly repainted in all-over poppy red, Alexander-bodied 49-seat Leyland Leopard **JHE 239L** had been reseated as a 53-seat service bus by the time of this May 1983 view in Midland Street, Barnsley. Originally numbered 239, this vehicle became 139 in December 1979 and **339** in April 1982 as a consequence of the reseating.

Below: Some eight years earlier in the same location, Bristol VRTSL6G No. **829** (**HWE 829N**), an ECW-bodied 77-seater, was just two months old as it awaited its departure time for Wombwell. Doubtless its youth prevented it being pounced upon and broken up in that notorious bus-scrapping centre. *(Both: G H F Atkins/© John Banks Collection)*

Above: Number **254** (**TKU 254S**) was a Leyland Leopard PSU3 chassis dating from 1965 that in March 1978 was rebuilt to PSU3E/4R standard and fitted with a new 49-seat Plaxton body. It is seen in Barnsley bus station in July 1978 loading for a limited-stop run on the X19 to Doncaster.

Below: In August 1983 No. **15** (**UDT 255S**), a Plaxton-bodied 49-seat Leyland Leopard, was at the loading bay for a National Express working. When new in March 1978, this coach was numbered 255 in the "dual-purpose" series but was renumbered into the coach series upon being repainted in express livery. *(Both: G H F Atkins/© John Banks Collection)*

Above: A striking demonstration of the success of the National Bus Company's policy of providing a corporate image for its coaches regardless of to which subsidiary they belonged is evident in this September 1981 Victoria Coach Station view. Yorkshire Traction's No. **59** (**DAK 259V**), a Leyland Leopard with Plaxton 49-seat coachwork, stands alongside an almost identical (though slightly longer) National Travel West example with confusingly similar numbering **359** (**KAD 359V**).

Below: New in February 1980, Leyland National 2 No. **208** (**EDT 208V**) traverses Midland Street in Barnsley. *(Both: G H F Atkins/© John Banks Collection)*

This and opposite pages: Livery - a combination of colours, emblems and lettering - makes the vehicles of an operator or operating group instantly recognisable. In early National Bus Company days it might at first have been thought that there was not going to be much variety. There was a lot, in fact, to keep the enthusiast photographer interested and busy, as witness these four pictures of the same Yorkshire Traction vehicle in - across a mere six years - four different schemes. As if that were not enough, see also page 48 for a fifth. In the view at Duple's coachbuilding factory *(above)*, 49-seat Leyland Leopard No. **252** (**PWB 252R**) is in brand new condition before delivery to Yorkshire Traction. The livery is that often described as "local coach" or "dual-purpose", with poppy red below the windows and white above. The wheels were a light shade of grey. The "dual-purpose" intention

is borne out by the full-length glass power-operated doors. This picture was taken in March 1977, but in the next view (<< *opposite page lower*), taken in June 1978, the vehicle had been repainted in the NBC's all-over white livery for express work. The main NATIONAL fleetname was in alternate red and blue letters and the YORKSHIRE TRACTION fleetname also appeared, albeit in much smaller lettering. This picture was taken in Llandudno, as was the next in the sequence *(above)*, this time in June 1980. The livery had reverted to the original, but with slightly different proportions of red and white, and the fleet number changed to **152**. Then in May 1983 at Pond Street, Sheffield *(below)*, the vehicle was in National Express livery and in another renumbering had become No. **12**. *(John Banks Collection [1]; G H F Atkins/© John Banks Collection [3])*

Above: A 1981 order for six Willowbrook-bodied 49-seat Leyland Leopards was reduced to two, the second of which was No. **162** (**KET 162W**), brand new in this June 1981 Barnsley bus station view. The remaining four of the order were bodied by Duple. The two Willowbrook machines did not last long in the Yorkshire Traction fleet and had been sold to City of Oxford by April 1982.

Below: Another brand new coach features in this view of Midland Street, Barnsley, taken in May 1982 of No. **165** (**OWJ 165X**). A Leyland Leopard, No. 165 had 49-seat coachwork by ECW and had somewhat inappropriately been rostered for duties on a Barnsley local service. *(Both: G H F Atkins/© John Banks Collection)*

Above: The Bristol VR replacement was the Leyland Olympian, the first examples of which were built at Bristol before Leyland closed that plant down. The Olympian was to be long-lived and No. **601** (**NKU 601X**), new in December 1981, was the first of them in the Yorkshire Traction fleet. The bodywork had 77 seats and was built by Eastern Coach Works. It is seen at Barnsley in May 1982.

Below: Number **652** (**A652 OCX**), a similar vehicle but new in May 1984, was leaving Barnsley bus station on a local service in August 1984. The livery included the logo of the South Yorkshire County Council. *(Both: G H F Atkins/© John Banks Collection)*

Above: In this August 1983 Nottingham Victoria scene, Yorkshire Traction No. **56** (**A56 WDT**) was leaving on the long journey to Paignton. A Plaxton-bodied 50-seat Leyland Tiger, it was one of four diverted from United Automobile Services that partly replaced two Dennis Falcons that were short-lived in the Traction fleet.

Below: The following summer, in September 1984, the same coach is seen on excursion duties at West Yorkshire's Harrogate garage. The livery had been changed to that suitable for *Rapide* services and the "cherished" registration number **YTC 856** had been substituted. *(Both: G H F Atkins/© John Banks Collection)*

Above: Outwardly an example of the standard ECW-bodied 74-seat Bristol VRTSL3, 1980's No. **924** (**HWJ 924W**) shows off the first post-privatisation livery of dark red, white relief and white fleetname lettering. This vehicle was a little unusual, however. Following collision damage, it was rebuilt as a convertible open-topper in May 1984 and is thus equipped in this May 1986 Barnsley bus station view.

Below: In exactly the same spot on the same day, Leyland National No. **229** (**LWE 229W**), a 52-seater that had been new in April 1981, wears what was to be a unique post-privatisation livery of red and cream with gold fleetname. *(Both: G H F Atkins/© John Banks Collection)*

Above: The second version of the privatisation livery is demonstrated in Barnsley bus station in July 1987 on a Leyland Olympian, No. **628** (**UKY 628Y**), a vehicle that had been new in July 1983. Its 77-seat bodywork was by Eastern Coach Works.

Below: On the same day a Mark 2 Leyland National, No. **228** (**LWE 228W**), seen leaving the bus station, has the version of that second livery as applied to single-deckers. *(Both: G H F Atkins/© John Banks Collection)*

One of the difficulties facing the modern vehicle recorder, whether the amateur enthusiast attempting to maintain a fleet list or civil servants feeding their computers with constantly changing data, is the reuse of registration numbers, a phenomenon that has afflicted the Traction Group fleets perhaps more than most. The number **NHE 340** is here *(above)* on No. **60**, an ex-West Yorkshire 1983 Plaxton-bodied Leyland Tiger, acquired by YTC in 1989. It was in Nottingham Victoria in January 1990, as was No. **52** *(below)*, with the same registration, in November 1994. This was a Plaxton-bodied 46-seat Volvo, new in 1988 to Shearings and acquired by Traction in 1992. *(Both: G H F Atkins/© John Banks Collection)*

Above: In pictures a little over a year apart, Leyland Olympian No. **669 (C669 GET)**, a 1985 ECW-bodied 77-seater, is seen with two quite different kinds of route branding. In this view, at Sheffield in April 1987, is was carrying lettering for the X90.

Below: The later picture was taken in August 1988, also in Sheffield, after the vehicle and five others had been reseated with 72 high-backed seats and given a new livery for use on limited-stop journeys marketed as "Fast Link". *(Both: G H F Atkins/© John Banks Collection)*

Above: Two Leyland National 2s received a livery for the "Fastline X20" service between Barnsley and Doncaster, for which they were reseated to 48. Number **262** (**TWE 262Y**), which had been new in October 1982, models this livery variant at Barnsley in July 1985.

Below: Plaxton-bodied Leyland Tiger 50-seater No. **59** (**C419 VDO**) was new to Road Car in 1986 and was transferred to Yorkshire Traction in 1988. In this picture taken in June of that year at Richmond Road, Skegness, it still had Lincolnshire's black and silver livery. (*Both: G H F Atkins/© John Banks Collection*)

Above: Number **104** (**RKY 773R**) wears the final livery/fleet number/registration number incarnation of the pair of coaches that began life as Nos 251/2. This is none other than our old friend, the one-time No. 252, now in all-over red "Coachlink" livery. It was working on hire to Rotherham Transport Services and was photographed in Nottingham in June 1988.

Below: Two months later, in more or less the same Nottingham location (Victoria coach station), Plaxton-bodied 50-seat Leyland Tiger No. **48** (**1901 HE**) was also carrying the "Coachlink" colour scheme and fleetnames. *(Both: G H F Atkins/© John Banks Collection)*

Above: Following the acquisition of the Gash business, a number of Yorkshire Traction vehicles were despatched to Newark, among them No. **455** (**XAK 455T**), a 1978 Leyland National 52-seater. It was photographed in a damp Newark bus station in May 1988.

Below: Numerous vehicles were cascaded from Traction to Road Car. This Lincoln scene shows native and incoming Leyland Nationals side by side, that from the then new parent company being No. **474** (**DET 474V**), another 52-seater, this time dating from 1979. It was still in NBC red livery with Yorkshire Traction fleetnames when photographed in July 1988. *(Both: G H F Atkins/© John Banks Collection)*

Above: Number **71** (**OHE 50**), a Leyland Royal Tiger with Roe Doyen 50-seat coachwork, was registered A71 WDT when new in August 1983. An impressive vehicle, it was photographed in Nottingham in August 1985. (*G H F Atkins/© John Banks Collection*)

Below: New in November 1986 as one of the first post-privatisation double-deckers in the Yorkshire Traction fleet, Metrobus No. **712** (**D712 NKY**) was hiding its age well when photographed in January 2006 on a Barnsley local service. (*John Banks*)

Above: This imposing Auwaerter Neoplan N722/3 with Plaxton 71-seat coachwork was photographed in August 1988 in Sheffield employed on *Rapide* duties to London. Number **92** (**C92 KET**) had been new two years or so earlier, in May 1986.

Below: At the other end of the vehicle-size scale at about the same time was No. **515 (F515 CDT)**, a 1988 Mercedes-Benz with a Whittaker 19-seat body. After a short spell in the main fleet it had, by the time of this May 1990 photograph at Newark, been transferred to Road Car with whom it is seen still carrying Yorkshire Traction's "Town Link" branding. *(Both: G H F Atkins/© John Banks Collection)*

Above: Wearing County Motors livery to commemorate the centenary of public transport in Huddersfield is No. **603** (**NKU 603X**), a 1981 ECW-bodied 77-seat Leyland Olympian. It was photographed in early 1983 in - appropriately - Huddersfield. *(John Banks Collection)*

Below: It is hoped that a succeeding volume will flesh out the story of the post-deregulation acquisitions in more detail and with more illustrations; in the meantime, the Strathtay connection is represented by No. **503** (**A114 ESA**), an ex-Northern Scottish 1987 Leyland Tiger with Alexander P-type 52-seat bodywork. It was photographed *en route* to Dundee in August 1995. *(Geoff Coxon)*

Above: The South Yorkshire PTE initiated "Nipper" services, using small vehicles, to housing estates. Yorkshire Traction operated a number of these in the Barnsley area, for which in September 1985 two 35-seat ECW-bodied Bristol LHS6Ls were acquired from SYPTE. The vehicles had previously run for Rennie's of Dunfermline and had been new to London Country in 1974. Illustrated is No. **599** (**GPD 308N**) at Barnsley depot in February 1986. *(John Banks Collection)*

Below: The same vehicle is seen in Lincoln in January 1989 after transfer to Road Car as its fleet number **108**. It was still in Yorkshire Traction colours but had had "Road Runner" fleetnames applied. *(Geoff Coxon)*

Above: Photographed in September 1990 with Yorkshire Traction legal-owner lettering, still wearing Tom Jowitt Travel livery but now officially Barnsley & District No. **L14**, ex-Midland Red **NHA 285M**, a 51-seat Leyland National dating from 1974, was laying over at Barnsley.

Below: Acquired with the Shearings Barnsley area operations in August 1991, No. **284** (**E24 UNE**), a 49-seat Leyland Lynx, was withdrawn in 2005. In this September 1998 picture it is about to enter Barnsley bus station on a service from Doncaster. *(Both: Geoff Coxon)*

Right: Number **901** (**E734 HFW**), a Volvo B10M.55 with East Lancs 80-seat coach-seated bodywork, was new to Lincoln City Transport in 1988 and transferred to YTC in 1993 for use on the X32/X33 Sheffield-Barnsley-Leeds-Bradford services. *(John Banks)*

Below: Among acquisitions in Sheffield were Andrews and Sheffield Omnibus. The operations were merged in 1995 as Andrews Sheffield Omnibus. On the left is former Sheffield Omnibus **1121** (**CRN 121S**), an ex-Preston 1979 Leyland Atlantean. It is overtaking 49-seat Leyland National No. **33** (**EFN 164L**), new to East Kent in 1973 but latterly in the fleet of South Riding, another Sheffield operator acquired by Yorkshire Traction and whose vehicles were absorbed by the Andrews Sheffield Omnibus fleet. The photograph was taken in June 1995. *(Geoff Coxon)*

Above: Barnsley & District (an old fleetname revived for the former Tom Jowitt operations) No. **317** (**K645 FAU**) was new in 1993 to Trent. An Optare Delta-bodied 48-seat DAF, it passed to Barnsley & District in 2002 and was photographed in Barnsley in 2006.

Below: Barnsley & District No. **176** (**L426 XVV**) is a Volvo B6-50 with Alexander 40-seat dual-purpose bodywork that entered the fleet in May 2003. The vehicle was new in July 1994 to United Counties and then ran for MK Metro, Sovereign and Huntingdon & District before passing to Barnsley. *(Both: John Banks)*

Above: Number **290** (**M290 TWB**), a 52-seat Northern Counties-bodied Scania, is seen in January 2006 arriving in Barnsley on a service from Rotherham once operated jointly with Rotherham Corporation. *(John Banks)*

Right: On the same service is No. **201** (**N201 CKV**), one of two 1996 East Lancs-bodied Spartans in the Traction fleet. *(John Banks Collection)*

Below: Former Volvo demonstrator **M630 NAC** became YTC No. **137** in 1995. It is seen on a Barnsley local service on 25th January 2006. *(John Banks)*

Above: East Lancs 39-seat bodywork graces this Dennis Dart SLF, No. **441** (**P718 WFR**). Dating from 1997, it acted as an East Lancs demonstrator before passing to Yorkshire Traction. It and similar No. 442 introduced the low-floor concept to YTC.

Below: A scene in the "new" Barnsley Interchange, described as an "interim" interchange by SYPTE, a few days after its 2nd January 2006 opening. Following Nos 441/2, subsequent low-floor purchases were to be based on the Volvo chassis, epitomised by No. **134** (**V134 MAK**), a B6LE East Lancs 41-seater new in 2000. *(Both: John Banks)*

Above: New to Trent in 1995, No. **358** (**N206 VRC**) is a 32-seat Optare Metrorider MR15 that was acquired by Yorkshire Traction in 2000. It is lettered for a service operated by Yorkshire Terrier with whom it had been on loan when photographed at Barnsley in January 2006.

Below: **YR52 YSY** with fleet number **227**, was in use as a MAN/East Lancs demonstrator before joining the YTC fleet in 2003. When seen in Barnsley in January 2006 it retained its demonstrator livery to which had been added "Travelink" promotional lettering. *(Both: John Banks)*

Above: Seen in Barnsley's recently opened bus/rail interchange on 25th January 2006 is No. **226** (**YT03 AYL**), which is a 41-seat East Lancs-bodied MAN.

Below: Number **610** (**N534 LHG**) is a Northern Counties-bodied 79-seat Leyland Olympian new to London Central in 1996. It is one of a number acquired by YTC in 2005 who rebuilt them from dual- to single-doorway specification before putting them into service in a new livery that seems to be a revival of the post-NBC scheme. *(Both: John Banks)*

Above: Scania OmniDekka No. **806** (**YN54 VKF**), new in October 2004, introduced a livery variation for low-floor vehicles. The yellow and purple scheme suited the East Lancs bodywork well. It was photographed at Barnsley in January 2006.

Below: On 25th January 2006 the first vehicles to be repainted in Stagecoach livery were in the Yorkshire Traction paintshops at Barnsley. Seen part way through the transformation are No. **212** (**X212 HHE**), an East Lancs-bodied DAF 46-seater; and No. **162** (**P347 JND**), a 35-seat Alexander-bodied Volvo B6LE, which had been new to Stagecoach Lancashire in 1997. *(Both: John Banks)*

Appendix - Preservation, Demonstrators, Trainers and Breakdown Vehicles

Upper: It is always gratifying when a company shows sufficient interest in its heritage to maintain in its fleet an historic vehicle. YTC's No. **492** (**HE 6762**) was a 1935 Leyland Tiger TS7 that was rebodied by Weymann as a 34-seater in 1950. Withdrawn and sold in 1958, it was reacquired in 1980, underwent a full rebuild and restoration and was licensed as a PSV.

Centre: **A451 LCK**, a Leyland Tiger TRCTL11/3R Van Hool 50-seater, was on loan from Leyland in August 1984 *(Both: G H F Atkins/© John Banks Collection)*

Lower: **H203 TCP** was a dealer demonstrator. A DAF with Ikarus 50-seat coachwork, it was tried out by YTC in April and July 1991. *(Geoff Coxon)*

Trainers:

Above: Larger companies usually retained examples of their own vehicles after their withdrawal from revenue-earning service for use on driver-training duties. These vehicles were sometimes extensively modified (a complete second set of controls including steering wheel was not unknown) although often the only change was the removal of the window separating the driving cab from the lower saloon and some external signwriting to warn the public. Typical of the genre was Yorkshire Traction's No. **836** (**BHE 766**), a 56-seat highbridge all-Leyland Titan PD2/1. New in 1950, it began its second career as a trainer in 1965. It was photographed at Rawmarsh in April 1972.

Below: Added to the training fleet in 1973 and photographed in May 1974, this 1961 Leyland Titan PD3A/1, No. **L10** (**VHE 201**), was originally No. 1201 and later No. 706. It had a Northern Counties 73-seat body. *(Both: G H F Atkins/© John Banks Collection)*

Recovery Vehicles

Upper: The AEC Matador military chassis frequently found use with haulage and bus companies as the basis of recovery vehicles. This ex-RAF example was fitted with a body built by Yorkshire Traction and given the fleet number **L1**. *(G H F Atkins/© John Banks Collection)*

Centre: The current bearer of the fleet number **RV1** is **OEM 785S**, a 1978 Leyland Atlantean AN68/1R, which was in Nottingham Omnibus and Road Car use before transfer to the parent fleet in 2002 for conversion and use as a recovery vehicle. *(John Banks)*

Lower: An earlier **RV1** was **FHE 800L**, a 1973 Bristol VRTSL6G fitted with ECW bodywork. *(John Banks Collection)*